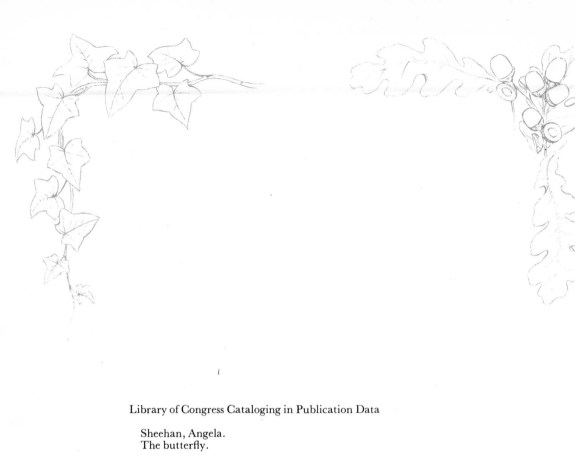

Library of Congress Cataloging in Publication Data

Sheehan, Angela.
The butterfly.

(A first look at nature)
Illustrations by M. Pledger.
SUMMARY: Presents the life cycle of butterflies as
they pass through the four stages from egg to adult.
  1. Butterflies—Juvenile literature. (1. Butterflies)
I. Pledger, Maurice. II. Title.
QL544.2.S48   595.7′89   76-49994
ISBN 0-531-09081-7
ISBN 0-531-09056-6 lib. bdg.

Published by Warwick Press, 730 Fifth Avenue, New York, New York 10019
First published in Great Britain by Angus and Robertson in 1976
Copyright © 1976 by Grisewood & Dempsey Ltd.
Printed and Bound by Mandarin Publishers Ltd., Hong Kong
6 5 4 3 2 1

The Butterfly

By Angela Sheehan
Illustrated by Maurice Pledger

WARWICK PRESS · NEW YORK

Drops of rain slid from the bramble bush. The butterfly clung to the underside of a leaf, keeping her wings well out of the rain. She waited until she could no longer feel the raindrops falling on the leaf.

Now the shower was over. The sun shone warmly and dried the leaves of the bramble. The butterfly could smell the sweet flowers. Stretching her wings in the sunshine, she flew from blossom to blossom sucking up the tasty nectar.

Other insects too were busy in the bramble. Shiny beetles crawled along the branches and stopped to eat the crinkly leaves. Ladybugs searched for aphids to eat. Bees and flies buzzed in the warm air.

As the sun began to sink, the butterfly flew from the bramble to find shelter for the night. She chose a large oak leaf. It covered her folded wings like a blanket.

Next day the sun was even warmer. The butterfly flew through the wood, looking for more flowers to feed on.

All over the wood, animals were out finding food or bathing in the sun. Birds tugged worms from the ground. Squirrels gnawed at nuts and bark. And spiders waited hungrily by their webs.

   As the butterfly went on her way, she
was followed by a fine male butterfly. He
was attracted by her pretty colors. As she
twisted and turned, he followed her.
Round and round they flew, like two
graceful dancers.

   After a while the female rested her
feelers on his wings. Keeping close, they
settled on a fern. Then, with their tails
gently touching, they mated.

Soon the two butterflies parted. The male flew off and the female fluttered to another leaf to rest. After a few hours, she felt ready to lay her eggs. But first she had to find a honeysuckle. For that was the only plant her young caterpillars could eat.

The sweet smell of the flowers led her quickly to the honeysuckle. She flew from leaf to leaf and laid one egg on each.

The eggs were so small and green that
you could not see them against the color
of the leaves. They would be quite safe
until they hatched.

Less than a week later, the tiny
caterpillars hatched. For their first meal
they ate up their egg shells. Then, each
day, they neatly chewed along the edges
of their leaves. After each meal they spun
a cradle of silk in the middle of the leaf
and went to sleep. They all grew fatter
and fatter.

The caterpillars loved to eat leaves but their parents could only eat nectar. As the summer days passed, the flowers began to die. The mother butterfly had a harder and harder time finding nectar. One day she grew too tired to fly any farther. As she rested on a leaf, a redstart flew down to catch her. The bird's sharp bill snapped on her wing. But the butterfly managed to tear herself away.

Weary from hunger and weak from her torn wing, she could only flutter a few yards. Then her strength gave out, and she fell dead to the ground. She did not feel the redstart's bill close around her.

Far away on the honeysuckle, the caterpillars went on chewing their leaves.

Soon the caterpillars were too fat for their skins. But that did not matter. They could simply burst out of them. For there was another larger, looser skin folded beneath the old one.

There was lots of room inside their new skins for them to get fatter. And they did. They ate and they ate and they ate, until they burst out of their skins again.

Once again they started to eat. But they could not go on eating and getting bigger for ever. Soon fall would come. And the honeysuckle leaves would drop to the ground. Then there would be no food at all for the caterpillars.

Before the leaves fell, the caterpillars had to make sure that they would be safe for the winter. All they needed was a snug bed that no other animals would notice. Already many of the growing caterpillars had been eaten by birds, wasps, and beetles.

The caterpillars made their winter beds in the same leaves they had been eating. They already slept in the leaves at night. So they only needed to make the leaf beds stronger.

First they lay in the middle of the leaf. Then they pulled the bitten edges of the leaf together and folded in the tip. They used silk to fasten the edges firmly round themselves.

But before they made their beds, they tied the stalk of the leaf firmly to the honeysuckle stem. It would be no use having a warm winter bed, if it dropped on the cold ground with the other leaves.

Warm and snug, the caterpillars went to sleep. The fall came and nearly all the trees and plants in the wood dropped their leaves.

A few oddly shaped leaves clung to the honeysuckle all through the winter. They looked so brown and dead that the other animals took no notice of them. They did not know that there were caterpillars sleeping inside the leaves.

After six months, spring came. Birds
sang among the trees and insects buzzed
in the branches. New leaves grew on the
honeysuckle. The sun warmed the sleeping
caterpillars.

One by one, the caterpillars woke and
pushed their way out of their leaf beds.
They had slept for so long, they were thin
and weak. They had had no food at all.

After a short rest, each of them found a fresh new leaf to chew. When they had eaten a little, they rested. Then they went back to their beds.

Day by day, the caterpillars grew stronger. But they still went back to their beds after each meal. Although they were stronger now, the caterpillars had little chance against their enemies. The birds that hopped about in the trees were hungry too, and the fat little caterpillars made a tasty meal for them.

The caterpillars that escaped the
hungry birds soon grew too big for their
skins. When they burst out of them, they
were twice as big as they were when they
woke up. But this did not stop them
eating. They nibbled their way through
leaf after leaf. As they ate they seemed
almost to turn into leaves. They became
greener and greener, and fatter and
fatter.

Later, when they burst out of their skins again, their bodies began to change. The spiky, brown spines on their backs grew bigger, and a fringe of hair grew along their sides. They looked very strange as they wriggled along the branches.

Now that the caterpillars were so big, fewer birds wanted to eat them. But a hedgehog that lived near the honeysuckle loved to feed on them. It could only reach the caterpillars on the lower branches. But every night a few of them disappeared into its hungry mouth. By early summer there were only five caterpillars left.

These caterpillars were now fully grown and ready to change shape completely. First they spun some silk and attached themselves to the honeysuckle stem. Then they changed into chrysalides. Each chrysalis was stiff and green, like a dry, crinkled leaf.

The chrysalides hung from the honeysuckle for almost two weeks. Their skins turned brown. But they did not move or grow.

One morning, one of the chrysalides broke open, and a small creature pushed its way out. It was quite different from the caterpillar that had spun a life-line from the stem two weeks before. The creature had a head with two feelers, a hairy body, and two pairs of wings. It was a perfect butterfly. But its wings were wet and soft.

Clinging to the honeysuckle, the butterfly waited as the sun rose high in the sky. Once its wings were dry, the butterfly would be able to fly.

Meanwhile, the other chrysalides had opened. The butterflies had spread their wet wings and the sun had dried them. Now they could all fly away to find some food. While they were chrysalides, they had grown long tongues. They could not chew leaves any more, but they could suck nectar from flowers.

The five butterflies flew off. Soon they had all found a bramble bush and settled down to their first meal.

As they fed, the sun went down. A cold wind blew through the woods. The butterflies could not stay in the open all night. So they flew off and found leaves to shelter under. The leaves would keep out the cold night air.

In the morning, the butterflies fluttered over the plants, sucking nectar from the the flowers. Sometimes they dropped down to drink from puddles on the forest floor.

Soon they felt the need to mate, as their parents had done one year before. Once again, all through the wood, the honeysuckle plants would be alive with tiny caterpillars.

More About Butterflies

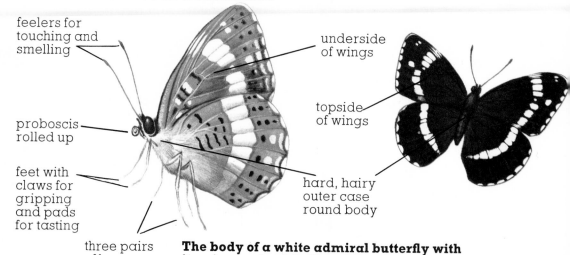

feelers for touching and smelling

underside of wings

topside of wings

proboscis rolled up

feet with claws for gripping and pads for tasting

three pairs of legs

hard, hairy outer case round body

The body of a white admiral butterfly with its wings raised (left) and its wings down (right)

A magnified photograph of the scales on a butterfly's wings

Beautiful Butterflies

Butterflies are the most beautiful insects. There are many, many different kinds and they live in all parts of the world. The butterfly in the story is the white admiral. It lives in Europe.

Scaly Wings

If you look at a butterfly's wings through a microscope, you will see that they are made of thousands of tiny "scales". The scales give the wings their color.

Butterflies smell with their feelers. They cannot see shapes clearly with their eyes but they can sense movement.

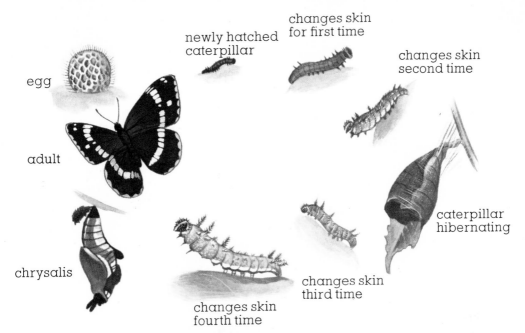

egg

newly hatched caterpillar

changes skin for first time

changes skin second time

adult

caterpillar hibernating

chrysalis

changes skin fourth time

changes skin third time

The life history of the white admiral

Nectar Drinkers

Butterflies feed on nectar. They have a special "tongue" for reaching into flowers. It is called a proboscis. The proboscis is a long tube like a drinking straw. The butterfly rolls it up under its head when it is not feeding.

The butterfly cannot taste with its proboscis. Instead it tastes with special pads on its feet.

Food

White admiral caterpillars eat only honeysuckle leaves. Other kinds of caterpillar can also feed on only one, or sometimes two, particular food plants. The monarch butterfly caterpillar feeds on milkweed plants.

Life in Stages

All butterflies go through four stages – egg, caterpillar, chrysalis (pupa), and adult. In hot parts of the world some kinds go from egg to butterfly in less than three weeks. The white admiral and many other butterflies take about a year to go through all their stages.

Most butterflies spend the winter as eggs or chrysalides. The white admiral is unusual. It hibernates while it is a caterpillar.